Snapshots

EXPLOSIONS

Sue Graves

D1143641

RISING STARS

Rising Stars UK Ltd.
22 Grafton Street, London W1S 4EX
www.risingstars-uk.com

NASEN House, 4/5 Amber Business Village, Amber Close, Amington, Tamworth,
Staffordshire B77 4RP

Every effort has been made to trace copyright holders and obtain their
permission for the use of copyright materials. The publisher will gladly receive
information enabling them to rectify any error or omission in subsequent
editions.

All facts are correct at time of going to press.

The right of Sue Graves to be identified as the author of this work has been
asserted by her in accordance with the Copyright, Design and Patents Act 1988.

Published 2008
Text, design and layout © Rising Stars UK Ltd.

Series Consultant: Lorraine Petersen
Cover design: Neil Straker Creative
Cover photograph: Alamy
Design: Clive Sutherland
Editorial: Frances Ridley
Illustrations: Bill Greenhead for Illustration Ltd
Photographs: AKG Images: 6, 7, 14, 17, 30
Alamy: 4, 8, 10, 46
The Art Archive: 6, 12-13, 20, 23, 24-25, 33, 36, 42
Getty Images: 40-41
Kobal Collection: 7, 10-11, 23
PA Photos: 26-27, 28-29, 33, 39, 44-45

British Library Cataloguing in Publication Data.
A CIP record for this book is available from the British Library.

ISBN: 978-1-84680-450-2

Printed by: Craftprint International Ltd, Singapore

Contents

EXPLOSIONS: THE BIG PICTURE

An explosion happens when something bursts with great force. Explosions make a lot of noise. They can damage buildings and kill or injure people.

FOCUS

Find the answers to these questions.

1. What do you do when you 'cook off' a hand grenade?
2. Why did the Chinese put cannons on a wall?
3. What is a tin fish?

ZOOMING IN ...

The deadliest
bomb of all.

Watch out for
booby traps!

Torpedoes home
in on their target.

Powerful pirates liked powerful guns.

Take aim and throw!

This bomb bounced!

Defusing bombs – a dangerous job.

CANNONS

The Chinese were the first people to use cannons. They put about 3,000 small cannons on the Great Wall of China. They fired the cannons at their enemies.

Later, people used huge cannons on land and at sea. **Merchant ships** had cannons – and so did **pirate ships**!

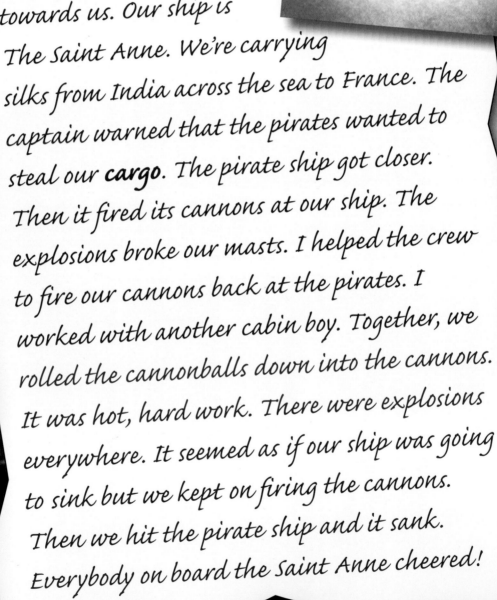

Monday 10th May 1718

This morning, the captain saw pirates coming towards us. Our ship is The Saint Anne. We're carrying silks from India across the sea to France. The captain warned that the pirates wanted to steal our **cargo**. The pirate ship got closer. Then it fired its cannons at our ship. The explosions broke our masts. I helped the crew to fire our cannons back at the pirates. I worked with another cabin boy. Together, we rolled the cannonballs down into the cannons. It was hot, hard work. There were explosions everywhere. It seemed as if our ship was going to sink but we kept on firing the cannons. Then we hit the pirate ship and it sank. Everybody on board the Saint Anne cheered!

Firing a cannon

It took a team of soldiers to load and fire one cannon. It was a dangerous job and the soldiers followed step-by-step instructions.

Instructions for loading and firing a cannon

1) Wheel the cannon into position and clean it with a wet sponge.
2) Add the **gunpowder**.
3) Push **wadding** on top of the gunpowder.
4) Put the cannonball into the cannon and ram it down.
5) Aim and fire the cannon.
6) Clean the cannon again with a wet sponge.

HAND GRENADES

Hand grenades are small, hand-held bombs. Soldiers carry them as part of their kit. Hand grenades are packed with **explosives**. Soldiers throw them when the enemy is close by.

Bilton News

SOLDIER HAS LUCKY ESCAPE!

Jed Brown, 21, is a soldier fighting in France. He had a lucky escape last week. His mother, Mrs Coral Brown, said:

'It's all here in Jed's last letter. There were some Germans in a **dugout**. Jed's **commanding officer** told him to throw a hand grenade into the dugout. Jed threw a grenade but it didn't explode. Suddenly, the Germans threw it back again! Jed kicked the grenade out of the way. It exploded but luckily nobody was hurt. Jed says he'll remember to cook off the grenade next time!'

THROWING A HAND GRENADE

1. Pull the pin out.
2. Wait a few seconds. (This is called 'cooking off' the grenade.)
3. Throw the grenade at the enemy – they won't have time to throw it back!

Pulling the pin

The first British hand grenade was used in World War One. Soldiers still use hand grenades today. This is what a British 36 grenade looks like inside:

KEY

1	Safety pin and ring	Grenade can only explode if you pull the pin out.
2	Striker	Makes a spark when it hits the special cap – the spark lights the fuse
3	Five-second fuse	Fuse burns for five seconds before the grenade explodes
4	Detonator	Sets off the explosives.
5	Explosives	The material that explodes

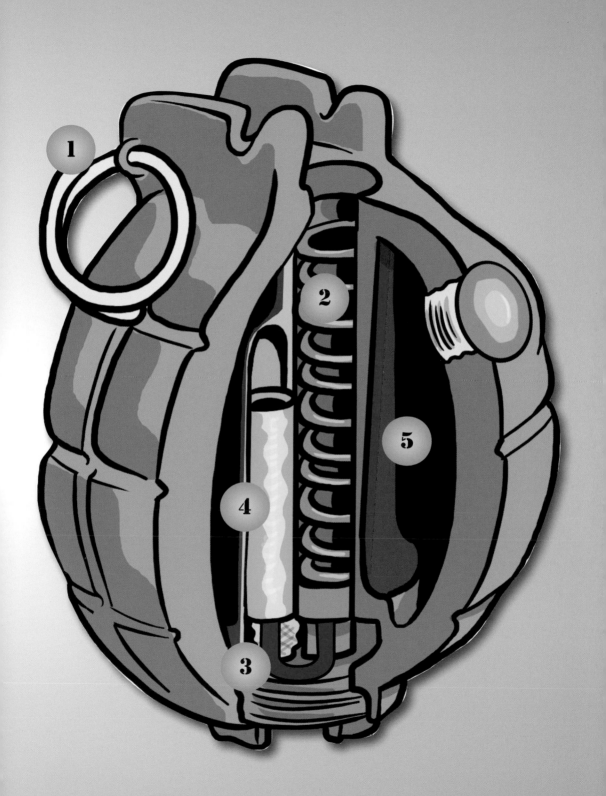

BOMBS

Many different bombs were invented in World War Two. There were 'hot' bombs – these burned at a great heat when they exploded and set fire to buildings.

There were also 'bouncing bombs'. British pilots dropped these bombs to destroy enemy **dams**.

The Dambusters Raid

PILOT 1 I can see the dam. Over.

Sound of machine-gun fire

PILOT 2 The Germans have seen us. They're firing at us. Over.

PILOT 1 I'm dropping the bomb. Bomb away!

PILOT 2 (*worried*): You dropped it too soon. The bomb's bounced over the dam. Over.

PILOT 1 Try to get closer with your bomb. Over.

PILOT 2 OK. I'm dropping it now. Bomb away!

PILOT 1 (*excited*): Good work – it's bounced down the face of the dam and exploded.

PILOT 2 (*pleased*): The Germans will be short of water for a

while. Over.

PILOT 1 And it will stop their factories working, too! Over.

PILOT 2 OK, let's get out of here!

The pilots get ready for action.

The dam explodes.

Bouncing bombs

The bouncing bomb was invented in Britain by Barnes Wallis. It was built to skip over water, slide down the face of a dam and explode.

The Dambusters Raid took place at night on the 16th May 1943. Nineteen Lancaster bombers were sent to destroy three German dams. The dams made power for factories in Germany. The bouncing bombs damaged two of the dams.

BOMB FACT

The Germans invented a flying bomb in World War Two. It was called the V1. The 'V' stood for **Vengeance**!

CLOSE-UP:
BOMB DISPOSAL

A bomb that hasn't exploded is very dangerous. Special bomb disposal teams are called in to **defuse** bombs. Bomb disposal experts often defuse bombs by hand.

Bomb disposal teams can also defuse bombs by **remote control**. This is safer for the team. They use a remote control vehicle.

TORPEDOES

Captain David Bushell invented the first torpedo in 1776. Torpedoes were widely used in the First World War. A torpedo is shot under the sea to hit a ship or a submarine. It explodes when it hits its target.

Falklands War 1982

Report on the sinking of the *General Belgrano* – 2nd May 1982

Report by Dan Green – British submariner

I was on duty when an Argentine ship was spotted. It was the *General Belgrano*. We got orders to attack the ship. We attacked it with torpedoes from our submarine. Two of our tigerfish torpedoes hit the *General Belgrano*. I saw lots of explosions coming from the ship where the torpedoes had struck. The *General Belgrano* began to sink. I found out that there were about 1,000 people on board. I also found out that many people were killed. Some people escaped in lifeboats but the seas were cold and there were high waves. We saw five Argentine warships looking for survivors. I don't know how many people survived.

Daily Mail

MONDAY, MAY 16, 1982   17p

ANDREW ALEXANDER SEE PAGE SIX

Mail Picture Exclusive

DEATH OF THE BELGRANO

THIS is the General Belgrano sinking in the South Atlantic, torpedoed by a British submarine. The 13,000-ton Argentine cruiser is going down by the stern and listing to port, sliding to join the wrecks of centuries more than a mile beneath the vicious sea east of Cape Horn. The moment any ship sinks—whatever the cause it may have died for—is one of desperate sadness. This classic picture, freeze-framing that moment, was taken from a lifeboat by a member of the Belgrano's crew. The lifeboat's plastic hood, to give some protection against the appalling weather, can be seen in the left foreground. There are more lifeboats in the water, distinguished by their hoods, bright red to help rescuers find them. And behind, the big ship herself, silhouetting the 1950s technology that can do nothing for her now and the guns that will fire no more salvoes. The Belgrano, when she was the U.S. Navy cruiser Phoenix, survived Pearl Harbour. The moment she made history on her own account—sunk with the loss of at least 368 men—was to come nearly 41 years later in a different conflict and a different world.   MORE EXCLUSIVE PICTURES are on Pages Two and Three.

INSIDE: Mail Diary 15; TV, Mail 18; Letters, Stars, & Strips 27; City 24; Peter Crossland 25; Classified, Adverts 24, 26

33

Tin fish

The torpedo was named after an electric ray fish. Torpedoes are sometimes called tin fish.

A torpedo is a large tube with a warhead inside. The tube carries the warhead to its target. When the tube hits the target the **warhead** explodes. The inside of a torpedo looks like this:

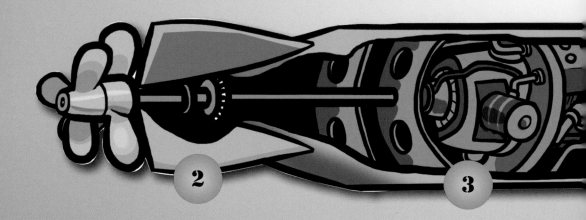

1	Control section	Directs the torpedo to its target
2	Rudder	Helps to steer the torpedo towards its target
3	Motor	Powers the torpedo through the water
4	Warhead	Explodes when the torpedo hits its target
5	Detonator	Sets off the explosive in the warhead

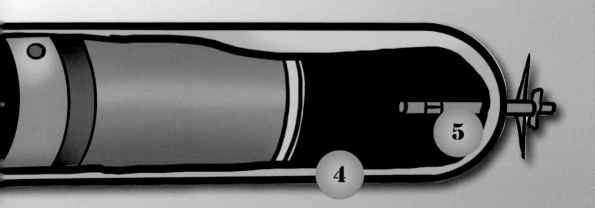

LANDMINES

A landmine is a bomb that's buried in the ground. It explodes when somebody or something moves over it. People lay landmines under big areas of ground called minefields. Many people want to ban landmines. They injure and kill innocent people long after a war is over.

Angola,
Africa

15th January 1997

Dear Grandfather,

Today Princess Diana from England came to the hospital. She stood by my bed and spoke to me. She asked me how I had lost my leg. I told her about the landmines in our country. I told her that I had been playing with my cousins in the field.

Suddenly I felt a big explosion under my feet. The explosion threw me into the air. I must have blacked out. When I came round, I heard my cousins screaming and crying because I had lost my leg.

Princess Diana said she was very sad about the landmines. She said that she wants to stop countries laying landmines. I hope she can do this!

Your loving granddaughter,

Anna

Clearing minefields

There are many landmines buried all over the world. Clearing landmines is a slow and dangerous job. Some minefields have maps to show where the landmines are and these are easier to clear. But many minefields don't have maps.

This is a landmine clearing tank. It has metal rollers that beat the earth in front of it. If there is a landmine under the earth it will blow up.

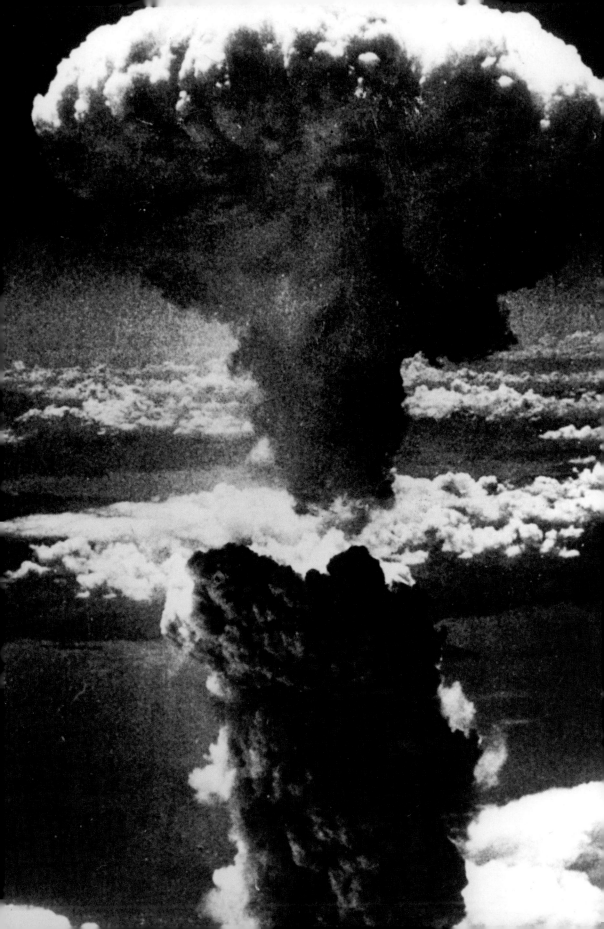

ATOM BOMBS

Atom bombs make more powerful explosions than any other bombs. One atom bomb can kill thousands of people. An atom bomb explosion gives off **radiation**. The radiation harms people for years after the explosion.

May 1960

Hi Mike,

I went to a Ban the Bomb rally last week. People from all over the world were protesting. Many of them are students like me. I really wanted to be here. I want to tell people how dangerous atom bombs are. We saw how much damage atom bombs did in Japan in World War Two. People in Japan are still dying from the effects of those bombs.

Why don't you come with me to the next Ban the Bomb rally? The more people that protest about atom bombs, the better.

From Jenny

Mr M Evans
3, Grove Street
Boxton
Boxshire
BX7 2HP

Atom bombs in World War Two

In 1945, the Allies dropped atom bombs on Japan because they wanted Japan to surrender.

The first atom bomb was called Little Boy. It was dropped on Hiroshima on 6th August. It killed 138,661 people but Japan didn't surrender.

Nagasaki after the atom bomb

ATOM BOMB FACT

Little Boy was 2,000 times more powerful than any other bomb used in World War Two.

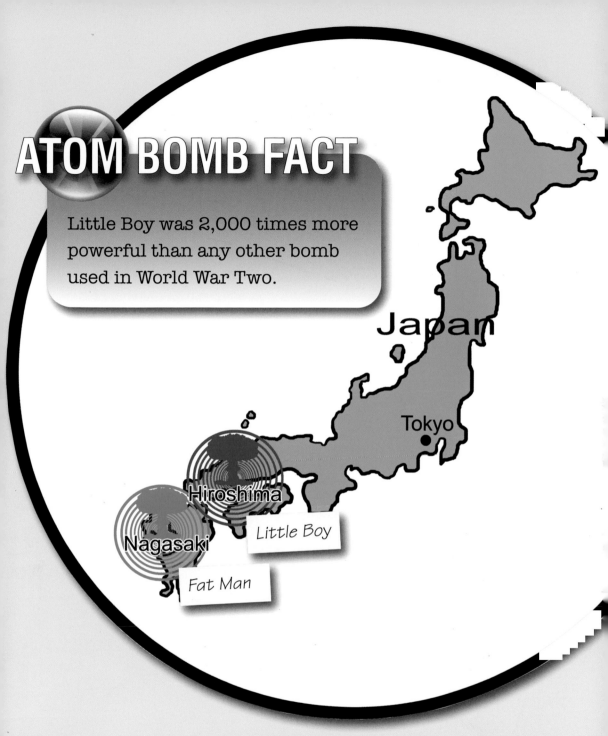

Japan

Tokyo

Hiroshima

Little Boy

Nagasaki

Fat Man

The second atom bomb was called Fat Man. It was dropped on Nagasake on 9th August. It killed 73,884 people and this time Japan **surrendered**. World War Two was finally over.

GLOSSARY

Atom bomb(s)	bomb that works by splitting atoms – this makes a nuclear explosion. Atom bombs are also called nuclear bombs.
Booby trap(s)	bomb that is hidden to kill or harm somebody
Cargo	the goods that a ship carries
Commanding officer	the officer in charge
Dam(s)	wall built on a river to stop water flowing by – dams can help make electric power
Defuse (defusing)	to take off a bomb's fuse – this stops it exploding
Dugout:	a hole or tunnel that soldiers dig in the ground as shelter in a battle
Explosives	material that explodes easily
Gunpowder	substance that is used for making explosions
Merchant ship	a ship that carries goods to other countries to sell
Pirate ship	a ship that belongs to pirates – pirates steal cargo from merchant ships
Radiation	a form of energy that can kill or harm people if they get too much of it
Remote control	making something move or work from a short distance away.
Surrender	agree that you have been defeated and won't fight any more
Vengeance	harming or killing somebody because they have done something bad to you
Wadding	a thick pile of something, like paper or hay
Warhead	the front part of a bomb that explodes

INDEX